THE CONTEMPLATIVE MORNING

40 Days of Reflection to Resilience

TRAY T.S. DEADWYLER

THINK FOR GOOD
STRATEGIC LEADERSHIP PARTNERS

Think For Good, Inc.

Copyright © 2024 by Tray T.S. Deadwyler
Published by Think For Good, Inc.

Printed in the United States of America.

Library of Congress Control Number: 2022918768

ISBN: 979-8-9877913-0-1

Printed in the United States of America

About The Book &
Guiding The Journey

This book is a guide to understanding and embracing the profound themes that shape our lives, from the words we speak to the love we share. Each page is designed to offer insights and practices that encourage reflection, growth, and connection. As you turn these pages, you'll be embarking on a path of self-discovery, learning to navigate life with intentionality, courage, service, resilience, and love:

- **Intentionality:** Considering the impact of our words and actions. Being mindful and deliberate in how you interact with others, recognizing that even small gestures or words can have a significant impact on those around you.

- **Courage:** You are encouraged to face and overcome your fears, especially those related to seeking approval or validation from others. This section challenges you to find your inner strength and to act bravely, even when you feel uncertain or intimidated.

- **Service**: The healing and transformative power of serving others. This section emphasizes the healing and transformative power of helping others. By engaging in acts of kindness and compassion, you can experience personal growth and fulfillment, and foster a deeper sense of connection with your community.

- **Resilience**: Recognizing the role of challenges in personal growth-viewing all challenges and obstacles as opportunities for personal growth. This section encourages you to see difficulties not as setbacks, but as chances to learn and develop, highlighting the importance of recovering and emerging stronger from tough situations.

- **Love**: Exploring the various forms and expressions of love, from romantic relationships to self-love, and the love found in acts of forgiveness and compassion. You are invited to open your heart to experiencing and recognizing love in its many forms in your life.

Consider this book as a daily companion designed to enrich your journey towards a more intentional and fulfilling life. Here's how to make the most of this book:

- **Start Each Day with Purpose:** Embrace each morning with a passage from "The Contemplative Morning." Let these insights be the backdrop of your day, infusing each moment with mindfulness and intent.

- **Dive into Deep Reflection:** At the close of each insight, you'll encounter thought-provoking inquiries. These are not just questions, but gateways to deeper self-awareness. Whether through meditation, journaling, or quiet reflection, engage with these inquiries to uncover layers of your inner self.

- **Actionable Daily Steps:** Every insight is paired with a practical action. These steps are your toolkit for weaving the day's wisdom into the fabric of your everyday life.

From small acts of kindness to moments of courage, these practices are your pathway to personal evolution.

- **Journal Your Journey:** Accompany your reading with a personal journal. Document your thoughts, emotions, and revelations to a chronicle your growth.

- **Reflect, Revisit, and Grow:** Regular introspection is key. Revisit the insights and lessons you've absorbed. Each rereading can unveil fresh perspectives, adapting as you grow in your journey.

Share Your Insights: Consider this book a conversation starter. Discuss your discoveries in group settings or with a partner. Sharing not only deepens your understanding but also creates bonds of shared growth and understanding.

About The Author

Tray T.S. Deadwyler is recognized as a seasoned, thoughtful, and reflective guide and mentor with over two decades of experience in fostering personal growth and self-discovery. His extensive journey, marked by a relentless pursuit of wisdom and self-understanding, community service, leadership development, and social change advocacy has led him to delve into a rich tapestry of ancient writings, life and leadership principles, and his own profound meditations.

Throughout his career, Tray has been deeply committed to exploring the human condition, understanding the transformative power of connection, and unlocking the potential within each individual. His approach is a unique blend of practical knowledge and deep introspection, informed by his rich professional and personal experiences.

As a speaker and facilitator, Tray has touched the lives of many, inspiring them to pursue intentionality and purpose. His work is rooted in the conviction that transformation and growth are accessible to everyone and that our collective well-being hinges on supporting these individual paths.

In "The Contemplative Morning," Tray distills his decades of learning and exploration into an engaging guide for those seeking a more mindful, courageous, and fulfilling life. His writing reflects not only his expertise, but also his passion for guiding others towards deeper understanding and heart-centered living.

Acknowledgements

Reflecting on the journey of writing "The Contemplative Morning," my heart is filled with profound gratitude. This book, a tapestry of reflections and insights, owes its existence to a host of remarkable individuals and divine inspiration.

Firstly, I extend my deepest gratitude to God, who has been the source of my inspiration and strength. It is through divine guidance that my meditations have transformed into words that I hope will resonate with others.

I extend my profound gratitude to the myriad of authors, thinkers, and leaders whose wisdom has permeated my thoughts and writings. Their words have been a beacon, guiding me through the complexities of thought and emotion, and their teachings have been the bedrock upon which the foundations of this book were built. To these luminaries, who have lit the path with their groundbreaking ideas and transformative philosophies, I owe a debt of gratitude that words can scarcely express.

My family, the cornerstone of my life, deserves immense thanks. Their unwavering love and support have been my constant source of strength and inspiration. Thank you for your endless encouragement and for being the sounding board for my countless ideas. Thank you for the daily reminders of life's beauty and wonder, teaching me about courage, resilience, and the sheer joy of being.

I am deeply indebted to my mentors – Kevin, Monty, Martin, and Preston– whose sagacity and guidance have been invaluable in shaping not only this book but also my personal growth. Their insights have been a guiding light in this endeavor.

A heartfelt thank you to my editor, Dr. Char-Shenda Covington whose discerning eye and thoughtful suggestions have immeasurably enhanced the quality of this work. Your patience with me and expertise have been a guiding light in the crafting of these pages.

To my friends and colleagues across the globe who have provided feedback, shared their experiences, and offered their reflections from the morning messages since 2016–your contributions have infused these pages with depth and richness. Your roses, thorns and conversations were invaluable.

And to you, the reader, my gratitude knows no bounds. Thank you for joining me on this journey of contemplation and personal growth. It is my earnest hope that the words within these pages resonate with you, offering guidance and light on your path.

With heartfelt thanks,

Tray TS. Deadwyler

Introduction

Welcome to "The Contemplative Morning," a transformative journey of reflection and resilience that I am eager to share with you. This collection, brimming with contemplative thoughts, ancient wisdom, and words of encouragement, is the fruit of a Daily Practice I began in 2016. Each morning, I would share my reflections with a circle of friends, penning down thoughts inspired by my daily meditations, a rich tapestry of ancient writings, and principles of life and leadership. These daily insights were my way of forging connections, offering a moment of contemplation to kickstart and mindfully approach the day. As the years unfolded, this practice blossomed, and from a trove of over 1800 messages, this first volume emerged.

Now, I have meticulously distilled these messages to bring you 40 days of contemplative insights, inquiries, and exercises-hoping to guide you on your path toward understanding, self-mastery, resilience, and transformation.

"The Contemplative Morning" is more than a book; it is a companion for your journey, a guide through the landscapes of the inner self. Each day unveils a new insight, a contemplative inquiry for reflection, and a daily practice to anchor the teachings in the fabric of your life.

Thank you for embarking on this journey with me. I encourage you to stay the course, embrace the process, and discover the transformative power that lies within these pages.

With gratitude and warmth and wishing you health and courage,

Tray T.S. Deadwyler

Contents

Intentionality

The power of words and the importance of being attentive to opportunities to inspire and uplift others.

Day 1

Today's Insights

Even a pebble becomes a heavy load when held too long. How much more is the anger, hate, fear, shame, guilt, grief, and unforgiveness you may be holding?

Just as carrying a small weight for a long distance can become burdensome, holding onto negative emotions over time can weigh heavily on the soul. A backpack feels heavier the longer it's carried, unresolved emotions grow heavier with time.

Contemplative Inquiry

1. What negative emotions might you be holding onto?
2. How have these emotions impacted your well-being and relationships?
3. What steps can you take to lighten your emotional load?
4. How can you prevent accumulating such emotional burdens in the future?
5. Who can support you in your journey of emotional healing?

Daily Practice

1. Identify any lingering negative emotions and seek healthy ways to process them.
2. Engage in activities that promote emotional healing, such as counseling or meditation.
3. Practice forgiveness, both for yourself and others.

Day 2

Today's Insights

Our prayers to be more patient, to be more courageous, and to be more peaceful are also prayers for situations and conditions that allow us to be such. The gift has been granted, but how does one know their strength until it is tested?

Just as a blacksmith tests the strength of metal through fire, our prayers for growth are often tested through life's challenges. And like a potter molding clay under specific conditions to achieve a desired shape, our prayers shape our circumstances to mold our virtues.

Contemplative Inquiry

1. How have your prayers for growth been tested in the past?
2. How do you prepare yourself for these tests and challenges?
3. How has your faith been strengthened through these experiences?
4. What lessons have you learned from these tests?
5. How can you support others as they navigate their own tests and challenges?

Daily Practice

1. Reflect on past situations where your prayers were tested.
2. Engage in spiritual practices that strengthen your resilience and faith.
3. Share your experiences and lessons learned with others.

Day 3

Today's Insights

The more truth, grace, and mercy we allow for our life, the more of the same we can allow for others.

Just as a tree's roots nourish its branches, the virtues we cultivate within ourselves extend to those we lead.

As a well-nourished tree provides shade and fruit for others, the virtues we cultivate benefit those around us.

Contemplative Inquiry

1. How do you currently embody truth, grace, and mercy in your leadership?
2. How can you better extend these virtues to those you lead?
3. What challenges do you face in practicing these virtues in leadership?

Daily Practice

1. Reflect on your leadership style and the virtues you embody.
2. Seek feedback from peers or subordinates on areas of improvement.
3. Engage in leadership training or workshops to enhance these virtues.

Day 4

Today's Insights

Either we begin seeing God in all things, or we risk losing the ability to see God in anything. We cannot allow God to be omnipresent when we prefer it. God reserves the right to be God, without our permission.

Just as a prism reveals the spectrum of colors in light, recognizing the divine in all things reveals the spectrum of God's presence.

As a mosaic is made of countless pieces, recognize the divine in each fragment of life.

Contemplative Inquiry

1. How do you currently perceive the divine in your life?
2. Are there areas where you've limited your recognition of the divine?
3. How can you expand your spiritual awareness to see the divine in all things?

Daily Practice

1. Engage in spiritual practices that foster a sense of connection to all things.
2. Reflect on moments when you've limited your perception of the divine.
3. Seek to cultivate an open heart and mind to the omnipresence of the divine.

Day 5

Today's Insights

Your life needs your full attention and intention.

Just as a gardener attentively nurtures each plant for it to flourish, your life requires your dedicated care and intention for growth.

As a craftsman meticulously shapes each creation, give your life the same level of dedication and purposeful intent.

Contemplative Inquiry

1. How do you currently set intentions for your life?
2. Can you identify areas where your attention may be divided or lacking?
3. How do your daily actions reflect your life's intentions?
4. What practices help you stay aligned with your life's purpose?
5. How can you inspire others to live with attention and intention?

Daily Practice

1. Set clear intentions for your day-to-day activities.
2. Prioritize tasks and activities that align with your life's purpose.
3. Reflect regularly on whether your actions align with your intentions.

Day 6

Today's Insights

May your daily habits align with your future hopes. Ask yourself if your present proclivities are pursuant to the purpose you seek. Act accordingly today.

A ship's daily course adjustments ensure it reaches its distant destination, your daily habits should align with your long-term aspirations.

In the manner a gardener plants seeds today for tomorrow's bloom, ensure your daily actions are seeds for your future aspirations.

Contemplative Inquiry

1. How do your daily habits currently support or hinder your future aspirations?
2. Can you identify any habits that might be detracting from your long-term goals?
3. How do you ensure that your daily actions align with your purpose?
4. What strategies or tools help you stay on track with your aspirations?
5. How can you inspire others to align their daily habits with their future hopes?

Daily Practice

1. Review your long-term goals and assess if your daily habits support them.
2. Make a list of habits that need to be cultivated or discarded to align with your aspirations.
3. Seek feedback from mentors or peers on aligning daily actions with long-term goals.

Day 7

Today's Insights

Excess turns all gifts into curses. Be cognizant of our proclivities and how they may produce self-serving addictions.

Just as an overflowing cup spills its contents, excessive indulgence, in any gift, can lead to unintended consequences. As a river can nourish lands but flood them if unchecked, even gifts can become curses when taken to extremes.

Contemplative Inquiry

1. How do you define excess in various areas of your life?
2. Can you recall a time when indulgence led to negative consequences?
3. How do you maintain balance and moderation in your daily activities?
4. What strategies help you avoid the pitfalls of excess?
5. How can you encourage others to embrace moderation and balance?

Daily Practice

1. Reflect on areas of your life where moderation might be lacking.
2. Seek feedback from trusted peers or mentors on potential areas of excess.
3. Set boundaries and limits to ensure balance in various aspects of life.

Day 8

Today's Insights

Let us ensure that our pursuits of truth are not merely veiled pursuits of control. It is an illusion of accession spiraling into an abyss.

Mirages do not only appear in the desert. What can sometimes appear real to us could be but an illusion. Our pursuits for control, masked as truth, can lead us far astray and away from genuine understanding.

Contemplative Inquiry

1. How do you differentiate between genuine pursuits of truth and veiled pursuits of control?
2. Can you recall a time when your pursuit of control led to unintended consequences?
3. How do you ensure that your intentions are aligned with genuine understanding?
4. What practices or habits help you stay grounded in truth?
5. How can you encourage others to seek truth with genuine intentions?

Daily Practice

1. Reflect on your motivations behind seeking truth or knowledge.
2. Challenge any tendencies to control or dominate situations or people.
3. Seek genuine understanding and connection in your pursuits.

Day 9

Today's Insights

Your movement toward truth and freedom always begins within, at the core of who you are.

If you are challenged today, come back to the center, your core. You will find rest and freedom unattainable through devices and facades. A tree's strength and stability come from its deep roots, our true strength and authenticity come from our inner core.

Contemplative Inquiry

1. How do you define your core or center?
2. In moments of challenge or doubt, how do you reconnect with your true self?
3. How do external influences or pressures impact your sense of authenticity?
4. What practices or habits help you maintain a strong connection to your core?
5. How do you differentiate between your true self and external facades?

Daily Practice

1. Engage in regular self-reflection to understand your core beliefs and values.
2. Seek feedback from trusted peers or mentors to ensure you're living authentically.
3. When faced with challenges, take moments of pause to reconnect with your inner self.

Day 10

Today's Insights

Time is a friend to everyone and no one. At times she can be forgotten, ignored, quick, slothful.... Hear me.

Treat every moment with her as a gift.

As we watch sand slip through an hourglass, marking the passage of time, we should value each grain, each moment, and make the most of it, for once it passes, it cannot be regained.

Contemplative Inquiry

1. How do you currently prioritize and manage your time?
2. Can you think of moments when you felt time was well-spent or wasted?
3. How do you harmonize the demands of work, personal life, and self?
4. What practices or tools help you make the most of your time?
5. How can you ensure that you're not just busy, but also productive and fulfilled?

Daily Practice

1. Prioritize tasks and activities that align with your values and long-term goals.
2. Reflect on how you currently spend your time and identify areas for improvement.
3. Set aside time for self-care and personal growth.

Day 11

Today's Insights

Those who believe that they have no need for transformation, need it most.

We should not be the same people we were a decade ago or last year. Remember, change is inevitable...Growth is not. Be intentional about your continual growth.

We know that a river constantly reshapes its banks, second by second, year by year- even if subtly. While the river's flow is inevitable, the direction it carves requires forces and interventions.

Contemplative Inquiry

1. How have you transformed over the past decade?
2. In what areas do you feel you've grown the most, and where do you see room for improvement?
3. How do you handle resistance to change, whether from within or externally?
4. What practices or habits have supported your personal growth journey?
5. How do you ensure that you're not just changing, but growing in a positive direction?

Daily Practice

1. Set aside time for self-reflection and personal goal-setting.
2. Seek feedback from trusted peers or mentors to identify areas for growth.
3. Engage in continuous learning opportunities, whether through reading, courses, or experiences.

Day 12

Today's Insights

Today, Choose your yes. Remember your why. Find your peace. Exceed your expectations. Love yourself.

This is your imperative for the day ahead. Just as a compass guides a traveler's direction, let these imperatives guide your actions and decisions today.

Like a map guiding a traveler's journey, may these imperatives chart the course of your day.

Contemplative Inquiry

1. What does "choosing your yes" mean to you today?
2. How do you stay connected to your "why"?
3. How do you find peace amidst daily challenges?
4. In what ways can you exceed your own expectations today?
5. How do you practice self-love on a daily basis?

Daily Practice

1. Set clear intentions for the day, focusing on what you want to achieve.
2. Reflect on your motivations and align your actions with them.
3. Prioritize self-care and self-love throughout the day.

Day 13

Today's Insights

May you enjoy where you are on the way to where you are going.

A grateful traveler appreciates the scenic views on a journey, not just the destination. Find joy in the experiences and lessons of your life's journey.

Much like a traveler who finds beauty in the journey's unexpected detours and not solely the destination, immerse yourself in the richness of your life's unfolding chapters, cherishing each experience and lesson.

Contemplative Inquiry

1. How do you currently find joy in your journey?
2. What are some memorable moments you've experienced on the way to your goals?
3. How do you balance focusing on the destination with enjoying the journey?
4. What lessons have you learned from the journey itself?
5. How can you inspire others to appreciate their own journeys?

Daily Practice

1. Take moments to appreciate your current circumstances and achievements.
2. Journal about the experiences and lessons you encounter on your journey.
3. Celebrate small milestones as you progress towards your goals.

Day 14

Today's Insights

Let us not attempt to push our real lives into the future. We have the right now for a reason. Let us be present in it.

Every photographer captures the essence of the present in a snapshot, we should seize and cherish the current moment in our lives.

As a painter immerses in each brushstroke, not just the finished piece, immerse yourself in the present, the canvas of now.

Contemplative Inquiry

1. How do you currently practice being present in your daily life?
2. What challenges or distractions pull you away from the present moment?
3. How has being present benefited your relationships and experiences?
4. What strategies can you adopt to be more present in your daily activities?
5. How can you encourage others to value and be present in the now?

Daily Practice

1. Engage in mindfulness practices to stay present. Consider a sixty-second mindful pause throughout the day.
2. Limit distractions that pull you away from the current moment.
3. Cherish and appreciate the experiences and people in your life today.

Day 15

Today's Insights

Silence becomes utterly absurd when the world's noise is praised.

Are you addicted to the noise? Consider today what you have not been able to hear lately.

Imagine you are standing at the edge of a bustling city, where the constant noise of traffic, chatter, and life is deafening. Silence would be surreal. But when you step away from the city and into the quiet of nature, you realize how much you've been missing - the rustle of leaves, the chirping of birds, the whisper of the wind. We often become so accustomed to the noise of the world that we forget the value of silence and the insights it can bring.

Contemplative Inquiry

1. How does the noise of the world affect your mental and emotional well-being?
2. What insights or realizations have you had during moments of silence?
3. How can you create more opportunities for silence in your daily life?
4. What have you been unable to hear or pay attention to because of the noise in your life?
5. How does silence influence your understanding of yourself and the world around you?

Daily Practice

1. Practice mindfulness and meditation to help quiet your mind and focus on the present moment.
2. Dedicate a specific time each day for silence and reflection. This could be early in the morning, during a lunch break, or before bed.
3. Limit your exposure to noise, whether it's from social media, news or other sources of distraction.
4. Spend time in nature or in quiet spaces where you can hear your thoughts more clearly.
5. Reflect on what you've been missing or ignoring because of the noise in your life.

Courage

Face and overcome your fears, especially those related to seeking
approval or validation from others.

Day 16

Today's Insights

Most of what is normal is familiar and causes no fear. This generally means that we have slowed our growth. How can one act bravely without the presence of fear? It is time to find your courage.

Just as a bird must leave the nest to truly fly, individuals must step out of their comfort zones to truly grow.

Contemplative Inquiry

1. When was the last time you stepped out of your comfort zone?
2. How can you cultivate courage in your daily life?
3. What fears might be holding you back from growth?

Daily Practice

1. Identify areas of your life where you've become too comfortable.
2. Challenge yourself with new experiences or tasks.
3. Reflect on past moments of bravery and draw inspiration from them.

Day 17

Today's Insights

Take time today and the next four to honestly answer this question: Am I fearful of becoming who I am supposed to be?

Just as a caterpillar undergoes metamorphosis to become a butterfly, confront your fears to undergo your personal transformation.

As a mirror reflects our external self, introspection reveals our internal fears and aspirations.

Contemplative Inquiry

1. What fears do you believe are holding you back?
2. How do these fears manifest in your daily life?
3. What steps can you take to confront and overcome these fears?

Daily Practice

1. Dedicate quiet moments for introspection.
2. Journal your feelings and thoughts about your potential growth.
3. Seek guidance or counseling if needed.

Day 18

Today's Insights

Let us ensure we are living the dreams of our lives, and not the fears of others.

As a captain steer by stars, not clouds, navigate your life by dreams, not external fears.

Contemplative Inquiry

1. How have others' fears influenced your decisions in the past?
2. How can you ensure you're living in alignment with your dreams?
3. What steps can you take to shield your dreams from external pressures?

Daily Practice

1. Identify any external fears or expectations influencing your decisions.
2. Reconnect with your personal dreams and aspirations.
3. Set boundaries to protect your dreams from external negativity.

Day 19

Today's Insights

Some of us will only believe our dreams when we see them. My prayer is that you know that you will see your dreams when you believe them.

As a gardener who believes in the unseen potential of seeds, believe in your dreams even before they sprout. A seed needs to be planted and nurtured before it blossoms. Dreams need belief and nurturing to come to fruition.

Contemplative Inquiry

1. What dreams have you been hesitant to believe in?
2. How can you nurture a stronger belief in your aspirations?
3. What steps can you take today to move closer to your dreams?

Daily Practice

1. Start each day by imagining your dream as a reality, feeling the success and joy it brings.
2. Write down one small step you took towards your dream each day, acknowledging your progress.
3. End your day with a reflection on what you've achieved and a positive affirmation about your ability to fulfill your dreams.

Day 20

Today's Insights

What you are most indignant about may be what you are called to change the most. Be brave in this moment.

Just as a fire alarm signals a potential danger, your feelings of indignation can be an alert to areas needing your attention and action.

Think of a lighthouse's beam, cutting through the darkest nights to guide ships; in the same vein, your indignation can illuminate areas in your life or the world that beckon your transformative touch.

Contemplative Inquiry

1.   What issues or situations evoke strong feelings of indignation in you?

2.   How can these feelings be channeled into positive action?

3.   How do you manage and process these feelings constructively?

4.   What support or resources do you need to address these areas?

5.   How can you inspire others to take action on issues they feel strongly about?

Daily Practice

1.   Reflect on issues or situations that evoke strong feelings within you.

2.   Identify actionable steps to address these areas.

3.   Seek support or collaborate with others who share similar concerns.

Day 21

Today's Insights

Your faith is activated in the realm of unknowing. If you already knew everything, how often would you engage your faith?

Picture a sailor navigating vast, uncharted seas, placing unwavering trust in the stars above; similarly, let your faith be your guiding light in life's vast sea of uncertainties.

Just as a sailor trusts the compass in uncharted waters, let your faith guide you in the unknown territories of life.

Contemplative Inquiry

1. How has your faith been a guiding force in times of uncertainty?
2. How do you cultivate and strengthen your faith?
3. Can you recall a time when your faith provided clarity in a challenging situation?
4. How does your faith influence your daily decisions and actions?
5. How can you support others in their journey of faith?

Daily Practice

1. Reflect on moments when your faith was strengthened during uncertain times.
2. Engage in spiritual practices that nurture your faith.
3. Share your experiences of faith with others to inspire and uplift.

Day 22

Today's Insights

Be not afraid, even if it's the minority voice. Most of your heroes wore the crown of misfit. They modeled not just a difference, but the difference. We need to hear you.

On the coast, a single unique gem stands out in a sea of stones. Your unique voice and perspective can shine brightly amidst the majority. Again, be not afraid.

Just as a single unique note can define the melody of a song, your distinct voice can make a significant impact in the chorus of life.

As a lighthouse stands alone, yet guides countless ships safely to shore, your unique voice, though in the minority, can guide and inspire many.

Contemplative Inquiry

1. Who are the "misfit" heroes you look up to and why?

2. How can you cultivate the courage to voice your unique perspectives?

3. In what ways have you felt like a minority voice, and how did you navigate that?

4. How can you support others in expressing their unique voices?

5. What change or impact do you hope your voice will bring?

Daily Practice

1. Reflect on the unique perspectives and experiences you bring to the table.

2. Embrace opportunities to share your voice, even if it challenges the status quo.

3. Seek out mentors or role models who have championed unique perspectives.

Day 23

Today's Insights

Do not give yourself the NO before you ask for the YES.

As a child, we learn to walk by taking uncertain steps, we should approach opportunities with a willingness to try, even amidst doubts.

Much like an artist who must first face a blank canvas before creating a masterpiece, approach opportunities with an open heart, setting aside preconceived doubts.

Contemplative Inquiry

1. How do you handle self-doubt or the fear of failure?
2. Can you recall a time when giving something a try led to unexpected success or learning?
3. How do you differentiate between genuine concerns and self-imposed limitations?
4. What strategies or habits help you approach new opportunities with an open mind?
5. How can you inspire others to overcome self-doubt and try new things?

Daily Practice

1. Challenge any self-imposed limitations or beliefs that hinder you from trying new things.
2. Set a goal to try something new or unfamiliar in the coming weeks.
3. Reflect on past successes that came from trying something despite initial doubts.

Day 24

Today's Insights

Realize you have nothing to fear in hearing the truth.

Light reveals what's hidden in the shadows. The truth, though sometimes uncomfortable, illuminates understanding. As clear water reflects without distortion, hearing the truth brings clarity, not fear.

Contemplative Inquiry

1. How do you react when confronted with uncomfortable truths?
2. How has embracing the truth benefited you in the past?
3. How do you ensure that you approach truths with an open mind?
4. What strategies help you process and understand challenging truths?
5. How can you support others in their journey of understanding and accepting truths?

Daily Practice

1. Cultivate an open mindset to receive feedback and truths.
2. Engage in honest conversations with trusted individuals.
3. Reflect on truths you've learned and how they've shaped your growth.

Day 25

Today's Insights

Those who are held by a fear of critique, of success, of failure, or of accountability may have a deep longing to be knighted. Know that this rarely occurs, until today. Allow this message to be your call to courage! You have permission to move. It has been within you.

Imagine a bird never flying because it fears falling or being judged by other birds. It would wait and wait for someone to give it permission to take flight. Yes, the truth is, the ability to fly has always been within it. You too may fear critique, success, failure, or accountability, waiting for someone else to validate your worth or give you permission to move forward, but the power to overcome those fears and take action lies within you. This is your call to courage.

Contemplative Inquiry

1. What fears are holding you back from achieving your full potential?

2. How can you transform these fears into opportunities for growth?

3. How does it feel to give yourself permission to move forward, despite your fears?

4. What steps can you take to hold yourself accountable for your growth and success?

5. How can you cultivate courage in your daily life and actions?

Daily Practice

1. Practice self-compassion and self-affirmation. Remind yourself that it's okay to make mistakes and learn from them.

2. Seek constructive feedback and use it as a tool for growth rather than a source of fear.

3. Set personal and professional goals and hold yourself accountable for achieving them.

4. Surround yourself with positive influences who encourage your growth and courage.

Day 26

Today's Insights

Our level of faith, hope, and love is ultimately hinged on our levels of courage, patience, and temperance.

As the roots, trunk, and branches of a tree are interconnected and vital for its growth, our qualities of faith, hope, and love are intertwined with courage, patience, and temperance.

Contemplative Inquiry

1. How do you see the connection between faith, hope, love, and the attributes of courage, patience, and temperance in your life?

2. Can you recall a time when one of these qualities significantly influenced another?

3. How do you nurture and balance these interconnected attributes in your daily life?

4. What practices or habits help you strengthen these qualities?

5. How can you inspire others to recognize and cultivate these interconnected attributes?

Daily Practice

1. Reflect on how your levels of courage, patience, and temperance influence your faith, hope, and love.

2. Cultivate habits that strengthen your courage, patience, and self-control.

3. Engage in activities or practices that nurture your faith, hope, and love.

Service

The healing and transformative power of serving others.

Day 27

Today's Insights

We risk so much by not bearing the fruit we are designed to produce. The results of such may cause famine for ourselves and those whom we are called to feed.

Just as a tree that doesn't bear fruit fails to nourish its surroundings, not fulfilling our potential deprives both ourselves and others of the benefits we could offer.

Like a barren orchard that can't feed a village, not realizing our potential can deprive many of the nourishment they seek.

Contemplative Inquiry

1. How are you currently bearing fruit in your life?
2. What potential do you feel you have yet to tap into?
3. How can you nurture your growth to bear more fruit?
4. Who benefits when you fulfill your potential?
5. How can you inspire others to bear their own fruit?

Daily Practice

1. Reflect on your unique talents and how you can use them to benefit others.
2. Set goals that align with your purpose and potential.
3. Seek feedback from trusted individuals about areas of growth and potential.

Day 28

Today's Insights

The open hands of the giver are just as open to receive.

Seek out someone to bless today. Let you and I model a smaller but living version of what we seek for the world at large. May our example carry the message and methods.

Remember, the sun gives light and warmth to the earth and in return receives the beauty of the world it illuminates. Our acts of giving also open us up to receiving blessings.

Contemplative Inquiry

1. How do you balance giving and receiving in your life?
2. Can you recall a time when an act of giving led to an unexpected blessing in return?
3. How do you ensure that your acts of generosity are genuine and not driven by the expectation of receiving?
4. What does leading by example mean to you in the context of giving?
5. How can you inspire others to embrace the spirit of generosity?

Daily Practice

1. Identify someone in your community or circle who could benefit from an act of kindness.
2. Reflect on moments when you felt the joy of both giving and receiving.
3. Commit to a regular act of generosity, no matter how small.

Day 29

Today's Insights

Ever noticed how service to others helps to heal the heart of grief, focuses the possible, and even sparks joyous moments?

Just as sunlight nourishes plants enabling them to grow and bloom, service to others nourishes our full soul- bringing healing, purpose, and joy.

Service is an act of grace that enables moments of gratefulness when reflected. If you are feeling stuck today, think outside of yourself and serve. Look for someone to feed, someone to visit just because, or a child to read to, the distant friend that needs a shoulder. It doesn't take much; it just takes YOU and a willing heart.

Contemplative Inquiry

1. How has serving others impacted your life?
2. Can you recall a time when someone's act of service deeply touched you?
3. How do you balance self-care with service to others?
4. What barriers or challenges have you faced in serving others, and how did you overcome them?
5. How can you incorporate acts of service into your daily or weekly routine?

Daily Practice

1. Identify local volunteer opportunities or community service initiatives.
2. Reflect on moments when serving others brought you joy or healing.
3. Reach out to someone in need, even with a simple act of kindness.

Day 30

Today's Insights

One word of wisdom, one word of encouragement is sufficient, enough to satiate and pour over all those that truly thirst for it.

Do not miss your moment! We rarely know the true and full impact we have on one another. Pay close attention to today and the moments available therein. The right words, at the right moment, for the right people, will yield a great reward.

A single drop of water can bring relief to parched earth. A word of wisdom or encouragement can bring immense relief and hope to the one who needs it. Every interaction is an opportunity to leave a legacy.

Contemplative Inquiry

1. Recall a time when someone's words had a significant impact on you. What was said, and why did it resonate with you?

2. Reflect on instances where your words might have influenced others, perhaps in ways you didn't realize at the time.

3. Think about a recent conversation where you could have offered encouragement or wisdom. How might that have changed the outcome?

4. Consider how often you actively listen to others and identify ways to improve this skill to better understand their needs.

5. Think about your upcoming interactions and how you can prepare to offer meaningful words of wisdom or encouragement.

Daily Practice

1. Practice active listening to better understand and respond to others.

2. Reflect on the words you use daily and their potential impact.

3. Seize opportunities to offer words of encouragement, even if they seem small.

Resilience

See difficulties not as setbacks, but as chances to learn and develop,

Day 31

Today's Insights

Much healing goes unrealized because much of what we see is unfamiliar. 'Pick up your mat and walk.' The new will not look like the old.

A seedling looks nothing like the mature plant it becomes, your new self may look different from your past, but it's a necessary transformation.

As uncharted territories hold hidden treasures, so does the unfamiliar in our journey to healing.

Contemplative Inquiry

1. How do you typically react to unfamiliar situations or feelings?
2. How can you better embrace the unfamiliar in your healing journey?
3. What steps can you take to ensure you're progressing and not stagnating?

Daily Practice

1. Embrace change and unfamiliarity as part of the healing process.
2. Seek guidance or therapy to navigate through unfamiliar terrains.
3. Celebrate the growth and changes you experience.

Day 32

Today's Insights

There is no need to force the flow of a raging river. Be patient with yourself, your life, and others.

A river grows and flows and finds its path naturally, carving through mountains and valleys. We too should allow our journey to unfold naturally, with patience and trust.

Contemplative Inquiry

1. How do you handle impatience or the desire to force outcomes?
2. Recall a time when patience led to a better outcome.
3. How do you balance the desire for progress with the need for patience?
4. What practices or habits help you cultivate patience in your daily life?
5. How can you encourage patience and understanding in your interactions with others?

Daily Practice

1. Practice mindfulness and meditation to cultivate your patience.
2. Reflect on moments when forcing a situation led to undesired outcomes.
3. Celebrate the natural progression and growth in your life, even if it's slower than expected.

Day 33

Today's Insights

It's not that life has become easier. The truth is that you are much stronger than you were before.

Flex your muscles today in the areas of life where you have noticed an increase in strength and competence. Growth has happened and you should appreciate this realization.

Consider a tree that has weathered many storms. It does not become easier for the tree to withstand the wind and rain; rather, the tree itself becomes stronger, its roots deeper and more connected, its trunk more resilient. You, too, have grown stronger through your experiences and challenges. It's not that life has become easier, but that you have become more capable, resilient, and competent.

Contemplative Inquiry

1. What specific areas of your life have you noticed an increase in strength and competence?
2. How have your past experiences contributed to your growth and strength?
3. How can you apply your newfound strength and competence to future challenges or opportunities?
4. How does recognizing your growth influence your self-esteem and confidence?
5. How can you help others recognize and appreciate their own growth and strength?

Daily Practice

1. Take time to reflect on your personal and professional growth. Identify areas where you have become stronger and more competent.
2. Celebrate your achievements, no matter how small they may seem. Recognize your growth and give yourself credit for your progress.
3. Use your increased strength and competence to take on new challenges or opportunities. Don't shy away from situations that push you out of your comfort zone.
4. Share your experiences and growth with others. Your story could inspire and motivate them to recognize their own strength and potential.

Day 34

Today's Insights

Life has a way of building you up… from within.

Obstacles and challenges are non-negotiable, but are prerequisites to demonstrating the strength you need to conquer.

Just as a diamond is formed under pressure, so too are we shaped and strengthened by the challenges and obstacles we face. These trials are not roadblocks, but rather stepping stones leading us towards our full potential. They are the necessary fires that forge our resilience, determination, and courage.

Contemplative Inquiry:

1. Can you recall a time when an obstacle or challenge led to personal growth or unexpected positive outcomes?

2. How do you typically react to challenges? What can you do to view these situations as opportunities for growth rather than setbacks?

3. How can you apply the lessons learned from past challenges to your current or future situations?

4. How can you use your experiences with overcoming obstacles to inspire or support others in similar situations?

Daily Practice

1. Identify a recent challenge or obstacle you've faced. Reflect on how it has shaped you and what you've learned from it.

2. Develop a resilience plan. This could include strategies for stress management, building a support network, and improving problem-solving skills.

3. Practice mindfulness and positive affirmations to reinforce your inner strength and resilience.

4. This week, seek opportunities for growth and learning, even in difficult situations.

Day 35

Today's Insights

Be not dismayed by the tragedies, nor too proud of the triumphs.

The greatest stories, like yours, have both. Take on a more complete, whole view of your life. Truthfully, we know what IS, by understanding what is NOT. We understand the triumph because of our known tragedy. Viewing life, in this manner, allows for great balance. The balance enables great peace. Great peace is your protector and stronghold for a beautiful life.

A tree requires both sunlight and rain to grow strong and tall, our lives require both triumphs and tragedies to shape our character and story. Embracing both aspects brings balance and depth to our journey.

Contemplative Inquiry

1. How do you currently handle tragedies and triumphs in your life?

2. Can you think of a challenge that, in hindsight, brought unexpected growth or insight?

3. How do you maintain balance in your life, especially during turbulent times?

4. What practices or habits help you stay grounded and at peace?

5. How do you define a "beautiful life" and what steps are you taking to achieve it?

Daily Practice

1. Reflect on past challenges and triumphs, recognizing the lessons from each.

2. Practice gratitude for both the highs and lows, understanding their role in your growth.

3. Seek balance in your daily life, prioritizing self-care, and reflection.

Day 36

Today's Insights

Maturity has no definitive end, so every step forward is taken from a place of lesser or immaturity.

Remember to give grace to yourself, and to others, when growth is occurring. We all are in need of it even today.

Imagine a mountain climber, ascending a peak that seems to stretch endlessly into the sky. With each step, they leave behind a lower altitude, a place of lesser height. They are always moving from a place of 'lower' to 'higher,' but the journey never truly ends. Our maturation journey is a continuous process. Each step forward is taken from a place of lesser maturity, but that doesn't mean we are failing; It means we are growing. Grow with grace and stay on the journey.

Contemplative Inquiry:

1. How do you define maturity and personal growth?
2. How do you handle moments of immaturity in yourself and others?
3. How can you practice giving grace to yourself and others during times of growth?
4. What steps have you taken recently towards personal growth and maturity?
5. How can acknowledging the continuous nature of maturity change your perspective on personal growth?

Daily Practice

1. Recognize that personal growth and maturity is a lifelong journey, not a destination.
2. Practice self-compassion and patience with yourself as you grow and learn.
3. Extend the same grace and understanding to others as they navigate their own journeys of growth.
4. Reflect on your growth regularly, acknowledging your progress and areas for further development.
5. Encourage open and compassionate conversations about growth and maturity with those around you.

Love

Open your heart to experiencing and recognizing love in its many forms in your life.

Day 37

Today's Insights

Those who seek love may find it in the embrace of another, in forgiveness, in joyous tears, in innocence, in creation, in a dark hour, or even within themselves.

Keep your eyes and heart open today. Love is all around you.

Watch a sunflower throughout the day and notice that it turns to face towards the sun, seeking light and warmth. It finds this nourishment not only in the bright midday sun, but also in the soft dawn, the golden hours of sunset, and even in the faint glow of the moon. The seeker of love can find it in a multitude of places and forms, most importantly they find it within themselves.

Contemplative Inquiry

1. Where have you found unexpected sources of love in your life?
2. How can you cultivate more love in your daily life?
3. How does self-love influence your relationships with others?
4. What role does forgiveness play in your ability to give and receive love?
5. How can you express love to others in a way that is meaningful to you?

Daily Practice

1. Practice mindfulness and presence in your daily life. Pay attention to the small acts of love and kindness around you.
2. Cultivate self-love and self-compassion. Recognize your worth and treat yourself with kindness and respect.
3. Today, express love and gratitude to the people in your life. Small gestures can have a big impact.
4. Seek opportunities for forgiveness and reconciliation. Letting go of past hurts can open your heart to more love.

Day 38

Today's Insights

May our compassion never not wear a watch.

Just as the sun doesn't set a timer to shine, our compassion should radiate without constraints.

As the moon doesn't choose when to shine, let compassion be ever-present, not bound by time.

Contemplative Inquiry

1. How can you practice boundless compassion in your daily life?
2. Are there moments when you've limited your compassion due to time constraints?
3. How can you ensure your compassion remains genuine and unhurried?

Daily Practice

1. Engage in kind gestures or helpful acts for others, doing so without the anticipation of immediate gratitude or reciprocation. Focus on the act of giving itself as its own reward.
2. Allocate time in your schedule to assist or support others, allowing for flexibility. Avoid imposing strict deadlines on these moments, giving yourself and others the space for genuine interaction.
3. Think back to instances where you may have felt hurried or constrained while offering compassion. Consider what led to these feelings and identify ways to approach such situations more calmly and attentively in the future.

Day 39

Today's Insights

Think of your life as a song. Now, consider who may be listening.

You are modeling your beliefs daily with your actions and words. May the song of your life be a song to be sung by others as well.

The goal of the musician is to play a beautiful melody. The notes they play are not just for their own enjoyment, but also for those who are listening. Each note, each chord, each pause, tells a story and conveys an emotion. Your life IS a song, and your actions and words are the notes that make up the melody. May the song of your life inspire others to sing a similar tune.

Contemplative Inquiry

1. What values and beliefs do you want to convey through the song of your life?

2. How do your actions and words reflect these values and beliefs?

3. Who are the people who may be listening to your song, and how might you influence them?

4. How can you use your life song to inspire others to live out their values?

5. What changes, if any, do you need to make to ensure your song accurately reflects your beliefs?

Daily Practice

1. Reflect on the values and beliefs that you want to model for others.

2. Be mindful of your actions and words, ensuring they align with your values.

3. Seek feedback from trusted individuals about how they perceive your actions and words.

4. Use your influence to inspire and motivate others to live out their values.

5. Regularly reassess your actions and words to ensure they continue to reflect your beliefs.

Day 40

Today's Insights

Learn to distinguish the differences between what is weakness and what is wickedness within your words and world.

Hint: most is weakness. Consider this for those not-so-loving moments in your present, past or future. These are usually cries for help.

Gardens have both weeds and flowers. At first glance, it might be easier to mistake a young flower for a weed, or vice versa. But with careful observation, you can distinguish between the two. Similarly, in our words and actions and those of others, it is important to distinguish between what is weakness and what is truly wickedness. Often, what we perceive as wickedness is actually a manifestation of weakness or insecurity. When we encounter snide or snarky remarks, it's often a cry for help or a sign of inner struggle, rather than a true reflection of malice.

Contemplative Inquiry

1. Can you recall a time when you mistook weakness for wickedness, either in yourself or others?
2. How can understanding the difference between weakness and wickedness change your perspective on negative behavior?
3. How can you respond to snide or snarky remarks in a way that fosters understanding and compassion?
4. What steps can you take to address your own weaknesses and prevent them from being perceived as wickedness?
5. How can you support others who may be struggling with their own weaknesses?

Daily Practice

1. Practice empathy and understanding when interacting with others, especially when they exhibit negative behavior.
2. Develop strategies for responding to snide or snarky remarks with kindness and compassion.
3. Seek to understand the underlying issues or struggles that may be causing negative behavior in others.
4. Encourage open and honest communication to address issues and misunderstandings.

Day 41

Today's Insights

Laugh at the tiny voices in your head deterring you from compassion, courage, and connection as you would laugh at the antics of a child.

At times, we find amusement in a child's innocent mischief. Those inner doubts can be handled with a similar light-heartedness, understanding that these doubts are fleeting and not defining.

Contemplative Inquiry

1. How do you currently handle negative self-talk or doubts?

2. Can you recall a moment when viewing a challenge with humor or light-heartedness helped you overcome it?

3. How do you differentiate between genuine concerns and fleeting doubts?

4. What practices or habits help you maintain a positive mindset?

5. How can you cultivate a more compassionate and understanding relationship with yourself?

Daily Practice

1. Engage in mindfulness activities to enhance your awareness of your thoughts and internal conversations.

2. Whenever you catch yourself engaging in negative self-talk, consciously counter these thoughts with positive affirmations. Remind yourself of your abilities, achievements, and worth to build a more positive self-image.

3. Open up about your doubts and fears with a trusted friend, family member, or mentor.

Day 42

Today's Insights

Speak the language of your new location. Your new environment will require a new lexicon, labor, learning, and love.

Every true traveler learns the local language to immerse themself in a new culture and adapts to the new environment by embracing its unique nuances and demands.

Contemplative Inquiry

1. How have you adapted to new environments in the past?
2. What challenges do you anticipate in your current or future environment?
3. How can you better prepare yourself for these challenges?

Daily Practice

1. Take time to observe and understand the specific needs and dynamics of your new environment. Identify what's different or challenging compared to your previous experiences.
2. Dedicate effort and resources to learn new skills or knowledge necessary for adapting to these unique requirements. This could involve seeking training, reading, or practicing new behaviors.
3. Approach this new environment with an open mind and a readiness to change. Embrace the opportunity for personal growth and be willing to modify your approach as you learn and evolve.

Day 43

Today's Insights

Speak in such a way that others love to listen to you. Listen in such a way that others love to speak to you.

Just as a musician plays in harmony to create beautiful music, communicate harmoniously to create beautiful interactions. As a dance requires both leading and following, effective communication balances speaking and listening.

Contemplative Inquiry

1. How do you currently communicate with others?

2. Are there areas in your communication that need improvement?

3. How can you be a more active and empathetic listener?

Daily Practice

1. Consider workshops or seminars focused on communication skills. These can provide valuable insights and techniques to enhance how you interact with others.

2. Regularly practice active listening in your conversations. This involves fully concentrating on the speaker, understanding their message, and responding thoughtfully.

3. Actively seek feedback from colleagues, friends, or mentors about your communication style. Use this feedback to make informed adjustments and improvements to how you communicate.

Closing Thoughts

As you gently close the pages of this book, I pray that you embrace this moment not as an ending but as a threshold to new beginnings. The journey we have embarked upon together transcends the confines of these pages. Allow them to be an invitation to weave these reflections and practices into your daily life.

Think of the insights shared within as seeds sown in the fertile soil of your consciousness, destined to sprout, grow, and flourish. I know there were a few days that were more difficult than others. In the coming days and weeks, take another look at those insights, inquiries, and/or practices. Notice if anything has changed.

The path of self-discovery and personal evolution is perpetual. I encourage you to carry the thoughts and lessons of intentionality, courage, service, resilience, and love with you. Suffer them to support your compass, guiding not only your mornings of contemplation, but every moment. The quest for deeper understanding and fulfillment lies both within and before you, unfolding in myriad ways with each step forward. May each dawn bring fresh opportunities for introspection, learning, and transformation.

Furthermore, in gratitude for our shared path, I invite you to pause and reflect: What change will you implement in your daily life to embody the essence of our journey together? Share this journey with others, and let the ripples of your transformation touch the lives around you, creating a community of contemplative souls.

The narrative of contemplative moments does not end here. Join me at

www.contemplativemorning.com

where our conversations continue, be it through our subsequent volumes, workshops, retreats, or the digital ether, and we can further explore the art of living with intention and heart.

Thank you for allowing me to be a part of your journey. May each dawn bring fresh opportunities for introspection, learning, and transformation.

May your mornings be filled with contemplation, your days with purpose, and your life with the testament of a heart lived fully.

With deepest gratitude and warmest wishes, Be Well, Be Brave, and Be Blessed.

Tray T.S. Deadwyler

www.ingramcontent.com/pod-product-compliance
Lightning Source LLC
Chambersburg PA
CBHW021003150626
46549CB00012BA/986